21 Templates that Run Your World

Sue Wilhite

Positively Success

Cover Art: "Fortune" from Voyager Tarot by James Wanless & Ken Knutson © Merrill-West Publishing
Interior Images from Voyager Tarot by James Wanless & Ken Knutson © Merrill-West Publishing

ISBN 10: 0-9794410-1-3
ISBN 13: 978-0-9794410-1-1

First Printing: April 2007
Printed in the United States of America

Positively Success

1669-2 Hollenbeck Ave #119
Sunnyvale, CA 94087
www.21templates.com

Acknowledgements

Writing a book is a group effort; don't let anyone tell you differently! In the seven year adventure of creating this book, a number of individuals and groups have made a huge difference:

First of all, thank you to James Wanless, my teacher and mentor. Your creativity, passion, humor and generosity were fantastic examples for me.

Thank you to my spiritual home at UCM, where the book got started during one of their events.

Thank you to all the great people at eWomenNetwork and eWomenPublishingNetwork, without whom this book would never have gotten finished as quickly as it did. You women are awesome!

Thank you to everyone who combed through the manuscript, making it better and better every time. Any errors or omissions herein are purely mine.

Thank you to the folks at the San Jose Metaphysical Book Shop, who cheered me on during the final steps to the finish.

And, of course, a thank you for my mother, who always knew I could do it.

Contents

What are Templates?

According to Dictionary.com, one definition of a template is "a document or file having a preset format, used as a starting point for a particular application." In human relations, psychologist Carl Jung introduces the concept of "archetypes" that serve as templates for common human experiences and images. An archetype represents a fundamental symbol of common, cross-cultural experience.

Everything in our lives is based on templates. We use them to make judgments and decisions all the time. For example, templates exist for the words "woman" and "man." When you read or hear those words you automatically know certain things about them, because you have a template in your mind already set up with information. Some templates overlap. For instance, the template for "human" has certain common characteristics with "man" and "woman."

Horoscopes represent a particular and popular kind of template. Everyone wants to know about and understand themselves, and, more importantly, they want to know something about the people around them. Even people who "don't believe in that stuff" know what sun sign they were born under and something about its characteristics. More people know their zodiac Sun Sign than their blood type. Why? Because (at least until recently) their blood type didn't mean anything to them. Our Sun Sign gives us a handle on our personality and on what to expect from ourselves, as well as from our family and friends. For example, Virgos are fussy, Cancers are moody, Taureans are stubborn, and Arians are impulsive. Also, knowing our sun sign allows us to discover what might occur in our lives. That's why many magazines and newspapers print a horoscope for the day, week or month.

Another type of template, numerology, also uses our birthday to explain us to ourselves. Numerology is the study of the relationships of numbers with other facets of life. The ancient Greek philosopher and mathematician Pythagoras and his followers determined that each number has a specific attribute associated with it. In this book, numerology and the Tarot are combined to offer a new perspective on our inner workings and a way to forecast what the coming day, week or month holds for us.

I learned this technique in 1997 from James Wanless, PhD, the creator of the Voyager Tarot deck, and it quickly revealed to me that I was a Fool/Emperor. This powerful combination explained a lot about my behavior, such as why I was always haring off in different directions and why I was known as the "Queen of Non Sequiturs." Worried about my latest new venture, one of my friends asked her father, a psychiatrist, what was wrong with me. He replied "There is a professional diagnosis for what Sue has: It's called 'entrepreneur.'" You'll see that occupation listed under the section called "Fool at Work."

You can use these templates as tools to get know yourself, your relatives, your business associates (assuming you know their birthdays), and what to expect from yourself and from others. You might also want to interact with someone you know and then try your hand at guessing his or her template. If they're introverted, they might be a Priestess or Hermit; if they're fabulously successful, they could have the Fortune template working for them.

Each template used here also can be viewed as an archetype, because it evokes symbols from nearly every culture on the planet. Thus, you might think of the Magician as Loki from the Norse worldview, and Coyote from certain Native American tribes, but it is still the Magician.

We all express our template or archetype differently. At a recent party, two people possessed the Balance template. One was an event planner who expressed Balance by having things go smoothly for people at an event; she hated chaos and lived by lists. The other was a CPA, whose career revolved around balancing numbers for clients. How much more Balanced can you get?

The two places our personalities get to express themselves the most – in relationships and at work –are also where we tend to experience the most conflicts and clashes. Nearly every person on the planet believes everyone else thinks as they do. However, it's a pretty sure bet that no one thinks exactly alike. We can reduce some of the problems in our work lives and in our personal lives by recognizing different templates and knowing how to get along with them.

One more thing: while I have used some gender-specific references within the Templates, any Template can be either sex. In other words, a man can be the Priestess or the Empress with no loss of masculinity, and a woman can be Emperor (I am!) and still be as feminine as she wishes.

How to find your Template

It is easy to find your template, even for the math-challenged! You may have one, two or even three templates to work from.

First, add together the month, day and year you were born. For example, if you were born January 21, 1959:

1	=	The month (January)
21	=	The date
1959	=	The four-digit year

1981	=	The total

	Your numbers	The example
The month (1 to 12):		1
The day (1 to 31):		21
The year (4 digits: 19xx):		1959
The total:		1981

Now, add the digits of the total together.
(In the example above, 1 + 9 + 8 + 1 = 19)

Your sum-of-digits:___ + ___ + ___ + ___ = _______ (a)

If your number is a single digit (1 - 9), stop here. This is your Template. Go on to the next chapter to read about yourself.

If the number (a) is a two-digit number between 10 and 22 (as in the example, 19), this is your Primary Template - how you show up most in the world. Continue on to the next section to get your Secondary Template.

If the number (a) is a two-digit number of 23 and above, you've still got one more step to get to your Primary Template.

Add the two digits together (in the example, 1 + 9 = 10)

Your sum-of-digits: ___ + ___ = ___ (b)

If the number (b) is now a single digit (1 - 9), stop here. If (a) was between 10 and 22, this is your Secondary Template. If (a) was 23 or above, this is your Primary Template.

In certain cases (as in the example), (b) is still a two-digit number, then your final template number will always be 1, the Magician (1 + 0 = 1).

If your Primary Template was 22, that's special! Instead of following the laws of mathematics, your Primary Template number actually becomes 0 (The Fool). The Fool has been assigned the number 0 for centuries.

If (a) was 23 or higher, continue on and use result (b) as your Primary Template.

Let's work through a few more examples:

November 17, 1961

11
17
1961
——
1989 1 + 9 + 8 + 9 = 27

This number is higher than 22, so we just add them together one more time:

2 + 7 = 9 This is the only Template for this birthday.

December 31, 1999

12
31
1999
——
2042 2 + 0 + 4 + 2 = 8

The sum is between 1 and 22, so we stop here. This is the only template for this birthday.

One more:

```
   8
  24
1986
----
2018  2 + 0 + 1 + 8 = 11
```

The sum is less than 22, but it's still a two-digit number. The Primary Template is 11; we go on to add those digits together:

1 + 1 = 2

2 becomes the Secondary Template.

The Templates

0/22

The Fool

0
The Fool

The Fool represents the risk-taker, the one who goes where angels fear to tread. The Fool has the unshakeable confidence that everything will work out all right in the end. The Fool sees everything as an opportunity, and every recent acquaintance becomes a new best friend. The Fool creates success, because in the Fool's mind no possibility or concept of failure exists; the Fool always finds the silver lining in every cloud. The Fool serves as the Path Finder simply by going forward. The Fool is fascinated by anything new - an object or an experience - and will move toward them by sheer instinct. But the Fool also easily is distracted and can be led off the path at any time. The path forged by the Fool is unlikely to be a straight line, but it may be the simplest and easiest path to his destination. The Fool is incapable of sustained effort since sustained effort just isn't "fun."

The Fool's motto: "What's that over there?"

1

The Magician

1
The Magician

The Magician creates, transforms, manifests, and manipulates. The word "magic" comes from a root meaning both "word" and "hand." Therefore, the Magician is one who creates using words and/or hands. The Magician possesses the power to create, and when the Magician is in a creating mood, mountains move, tall buildings are as candles, and creating something out of nothing becomes child's play. Most of all, the Magician has a silver tongue with the power to convince others of his or her ideas and visions, thus bringing them into reality. The Magician can make others believe in his dreams or in anything at all. So, beware of playing the shell game with him!

The Magician's motto: "Make it so!"

2

The Priestess

2
The Priestess

The Priestess represents that deep inner knowing of purpose, order and the rightness of the Universe. If the Priestess had a sound, it would be the whale song, which only is heard by those prepared to listen in an extraordinary way. The Priestess sees through things, above things, below things, behind things. She may, however, miss what is right in front of her, for she is focused somewhere else entirely. The word "insight" was created for her. Little can ruffle the smooth waters of the Priestess – except perhaps being wrong. Depending on her degree of spiritual or emotional development, the Priestess may cause tsunamis or whirlpools to drown the unwary one who points out her error, or she may offer sincere thanks followed by a withdrawal to reset her inner compass and take account of her bearings. None are better than the Priestess as supporters for any cause or to boost your confidence, and none are worse as opponents or for delivering sheer scorn for anyone daring to pick the "wrong" point of view.

The Priestess' motto: "I know what I know."

3

The Empress

3
The Empress

The Empress embodies love in all its aspects. Fruitful and abundant, she symbolizes love of the Earth and all that reside on or within it. Full of compassion, she comforts and protects all those who need it. She is the source of all instinct to nurture and to care for self and others. The Empress serves as the "Keeper of the Way" (sometimes known as the Tao). The Empress cares nothing for differences in appearances or in opinions but works to find the correspondences and similarities in all things. The Empress is in touch with all that lives, and believes at a very deep level that all things are alive in their own unique way. The Empress represents growth, health and vitality. She can give too much and, therefore, must take care to maintain both internal and external boundaries.

The Empress' motto: "What do you need?"

4

The Emperor

4
The Emperor

The Emperor is out to conquer the world and may just charm you into letting him do it! The Emperor has a plan, an idea, a goal. Although sometimes others inspire it, the Emperor always puts his own unique twist on that plan. With a grasp on the big picture and the grand scheme of things, he leaves it to others to take care of the small petty details. If too many details exist and too few people are available to take care of them, the Emperor gets bogged down and frustrated and goes off to the next fresh idea that captures his imagination. The Emperor's projects tend to involve matters of the material world and improvements of one sort or another. More than capable of starting a spiritual crusade of his own if so inspired, the Emperor doesn't just rule, he leads. You'll always find him at the forefront of any group. The Emperor may be completely unaware of the needs of others, but, to be perfectly fair, he also ignores his own. Many Emperors suffer from burnout. The Emperor has a practical, utilitarian nature and only is interested in solutions, not problems.

The Emperor's motto: "Me first!"

5

The Hierophant

5
The Hierophant

The Hierophant or "Light Bringer" represents the spiritual teacher, the one in touch with the divine. Unlike the Priestess, the Hierophant prefers to share this gift with others. The Hierophant constantly seeks knowledge and compulsively shares knowledge. The creator and/or keeper of ritual or process, the Hierophant can get bogged down with dogma and feel confident in the rightness of his or her beliefs. The Hierophant is concerned with making sure everyone shares his "true" vision and can be intolerant or impatient with those who have a different path or belief system. However, his stubbornness can serve as a great asset, since once he is set on a completing a task very little moves him from accomplishing it. It behooves any who wish to change the Hierophant's mind to have their arguments well prepared. The Hierophant changes his mind only when faced with overwhelming evidence. The Hierophant does very little lightly or frivolously.

The Hierophant's motto: "Did you know..."

6

The Lovers

6
The Lovers

The Lovers live as two-in-one, sharing with each other, resonating with each other, distinguishing duality from singularity. The Lovers are acutely aware of contrasts: up/down, in/out, black/white, and are therefore exquisitely aware of the existence of the "other" in their lives. More aware of choices than any other template, some Lovers find making decisions easy while some find the task paralyzingly difficult, and some experience it both ways. The Lovers are more than capable of walking in another's moccasins, since they have the ability to see from others' viewpoints – sometimes to the exclusion of their own.

The Lovers' motto: "Who are you?"

7

The Chariot

7
The Chariot

Ride like the wind! The Chariot represents the energetic force in the universe. Sometimes it acts like a volcano, exploding outward in all directions, while at other times its energy is channeled and refined like geothermal geysers. If people with this template use the energy, it can take them far very quickly. If the energy uses them, however, they will get used up just as quickly. The Chariot serves as the motivator, the mover-and-shaker, the kick in the pants, $E=MC^2$. The Chariot creates a path by mowing down everything in its way and by doing so without waiting for anyone or anything. The Chariot cannot stay in one place for very long – every place is seen as just a pit stop at best – and will champ at the bit to get back on track if forced to tarry. The Chariot's challenge lies in balancing all that energy. To make the Chariot happy, give it a quest with no endpoint. The Chariot never sees barriers. For Chariots, the time is always now.

The Chariot's motto: "Let's go!"

8

Balance

8
Balance

Balance provides the way between. Balance poises on the knife-edge, rocking back and forth, up and down. And Balance finds those sharp edges the most interesting parts of life, because they represent the point at which the end starts and the beginning fades away. Therefore, Balance has nothing to do with duality, such as black and white or up and down, but everything to do with all the myriad ways in between, otherwise known as the "grey areas." At its best, Balance gives the illusion of stillness by maintaining micro-movements that allow it to experience either side at will. At the other extreme, Balance wildly flails its limbs, acting as if on a bumpy seesaw ride. It exhibits bursts of energy as well as major shifts in perception.

Balance's motto: "What goes up must come down."

9

Hermit

9
Hermit

The Hermit stays internally focused within himself and observes everything around and outside himself. Everything is grist for the mill – words and actions, shouting and silence, nature and artifice; the Hermit gathers information from everywhere. When faced with too much data, or simply when it's time, the Hermit withdraws to correlate, organize and integrate. Once done with these tasks, the Hermit communicates the new synthesis of knowledge gathered and shares the fruits of the mental harvest. The Hermit can possess the gift of making the complex simple, of organizing confusing data into something that easily makes sense. To the Hermit, doing so is as easy as breathing in and breathing out.

The Hermit's motto: "There is a season."

10

Fortune

10
Fortune

Fortune is like a wild ride on the most exciting roller coaster ever or like the most placid, uneventful, almost boring, time spent sitting in a boat on a still lake. Fortune represents the taking of opportunities when they come up. Always prepared for opportunities, Fortune watches the wheel turn toward him and takes from it what he needs, then releases it as it turns away again. If Fortune were to snatch and grab at the wheel, he would become frustrated and angry when he misses the mark or disappointed and angry when the wheel turns in an unexpected direction just as he grabs hold. Fortune represents a fundamental Law of Abundance: When you know you have it, then you do. When you focus on your lack, you are left with nothing.

Fortune's motto: "What's next?"

11

Strength

11
Strength

True Strength has a power that neither dominates nor represses. When Strength works from integrity, she can move mountains and change the world. The power that comes from Strength fuels a dream's manifestation in the world. Strength, when guided by wisdom, moves into new ventures as easily and naturally as breathing. When misguided or reckless, Strength seems more like a volcano, exploding and burning everything in its path, yet building new layers of land in its wake. True Strength stems from being grounded, from a serene awareness of Self.

Strength's motto: "I am that I am."

12

Hanged Man

12
Hanged Man

The Hanged Man, when true to his nature, has multiple ways of being in the world. The Hanged Man is characterized by his ability to sacrifice. Such sacrifice might be as little as giving away a favorite toy or as large as giving away millions of dollars to charity. For such a sacrifice to be meaningful, it must be given whole-heartedly and willingly. The challenge for the Hanged Man lies in not making such a big deal out of it that the sacrifice evokes guilt in others. Sometimes, though, the sacrifice for the Hanged Man is simply a shift in perspective. Of course, sacrificing a point of view can be the most challenging sacrifice one makes. Many people would rather give up their lives than their beliefs. However, the Hanged Man's creativity can be stimulated and grown by discarding old, outworn modes and seeing through new eyes.

The Hanged Man's motto: "I'll do anything for you!"

13

Death

13
Death

Death involves great change and transition from one state of being to another. When Death works properly, change simply becomes another part of life. Shed the old skin, come out of the old shell, and grow into something different and greater. Death's challenge: to honor all that has come before, without getting stuck in the past. You cannot afford regret.

Death's motto: "Live and learn."

14

Art

14
Art

The passion of creativity! Feel the fire of the crucible as an Idea is transformed, boiled down, refined, stretched, even patched, in order to become manifest. The Art template involves the process of making all dreams real. Art lives "in the zone" of creativity, where ideas flow and new patterns emerge. Native American artists of the West had a tradition of deliberately creating an imperfection in their creation to prevent the artist's soul from being bound forever to the creation. They understood true creativity to involve the whole being. The outpouring of the Self into creating a project contains both danger and joy. Art can get lost in the project at hand and may seem a little crazy, or at least temperamental. Art needs to breathe out, as well as in.

Art's motto: "What's new?"

15

Devil's Play

15
Devil's Play

Fun, fun, fun! Ride on the merry-go-round of your childhood for a day, and laugh out loud at the passers-by. Play hopscotch, Red Rover or tag but not Mother-May-I! Devil's Play never asks permission. The Devil's Play template at its best suffers no ties that bind; instead, he leaps out of the box and explores all limits. After all, the best experience of life indulges all the senses. However, Devil's Play many times can be found addicted to drugs, money, alcohol, power, sex, or other material things. It's best to avoid getting addicted to a form of fun and to avoid thinking fun is all that life offers, because those ideas bind as well. Life involves a full range of experiences, and succumbing to only one aspect serves as a sure way to lose it. Devil's Play must remain open to all the senses and get to know Life like a lover in a new affair who can't get enough of the other person.

Devil's Play motto: "Let's have fun!"

16

The Tower

16
The Tower

WHAM! . The universal two-by-four has just struck, and knocked you off your feet in some unexpected way. As you pick yourself up, the nearly-unanimous response is, "What happened?", followed closely in many cases by, "Why me?" The answer is simple: you were stuck and needed to get unstuck. Chances are good that you had multiple opportunities to handle whatever issue had you stuck — but you didn't. Now you got laid off - but the job wasn't right for you anyway. You got into an accident - but you ended up receiving some much-needed cash from the insurance company. Maybe whatever has happened helped you get rid of something that had served its purpose or helped you achieve a necessary shift in perspective. The Tower needs to pay attention to the status quo as well as to what can be changed by choice. It requires discerning what changes can be made in a controlled manner rather than by being struck by lightning.

Tower's motto: "What was that?"

17

Star

17
Star

When they are fully actualized, Stars not only can accomplish much for themselves but can help others achieve great things as well. The Star is not arrogant but full of compassion for those who are striving to catch up to them. At their best, Stars give direction to the rest, but do so from the place of connection to all living beings (and even what we think of as non-living objects). The Star radiates outward so that others may see, and joins with other Stars to increase the path's illumination for others. Being a Star involves accepting change, for every Star constantly creates and changes its own internal fuel. Being a Star means to accept and work towards your own dreams while also helping others manifest theirs. Dark Stars whine and complain and grow green with envy when others make progress. They absorb others' light as their own.

The Star's motto: "Shine on!"

18

Moon

18
Moon

The Moon represents the cyclical nature of life, the seasons of movement within everything. The Moon has more facets to her than nearly any other template. The full Moon gathers the tides and pulls them to new heights. The Crescent Moons, waxing or waning, represent the opportunity to build or a time to release as forces start to shift. The new Moon offers a time of darkness, tells of things hidden from and things in hiding. When the Moon fights against these cycles, she finds herself snappish and irritable. When she works with them, her life becomes full and abundant.

The Moon's motto: "Go with the flow."

19

Sun

19
Sun

Being the Sun means being free, being open, being expressive, being and having abundance, growing, and flowering. The Sun says, "Look at ME! I'm great!" The Sun shines light energy that fits into the smallest crack and penetrates deeply in all directions. The Sun reflects and refracts from millions of surfaces and textures, bringing rainbows of color into the world. The Sun sees all, shows all, reveals all, and goes everywhere and anywhere. Others both love and hate the Sun, for while growth and life require light, that same light also can burn or burn out. Not everything lives on the surface nor wishes to be revealed; some things prefer to remain hidden in the dark.

The Sun's motto: "Here I am!"

20

Time-Space

20
Time-Space

Time-Space has perspective in both of those dimensions. They take the 65,000-foot view, and find themselves most comfortable doing the long-range planning. Plotting out everything far in advance, Time-Space find it difficult to be spontaneous, but they are always in the moment. They saw it coming, and they will likely tell you so. When at their worst, Time-Space becomes paralyzed by the number of possibilities open to them and won't be able to make a choice at all.

Time-Space's motto: "Watch where you're going."

21

Universe

21
Universe

Omniscient, omnipresent, omnipotent: these are the characteristics of a deity. The Universe can have it all: full and complete emotional expression, physical health and well-being, mental clarity and creativity, as well as spiritual integration. Manifestation becomes effortless. External reality automatically reflects the Universe's wishes. The Universe forms connections, putting things together and finding synergy in all situations. However, because what he wants is what he gets, negative expectations become negative reality. It's almost impossible to convince the negative Universe that another, more-positive outcome exists.

The Universe's motto: "If you want it, here it is; come and get it!"

Celebrity Birthdays

**Former US President Bill Clinton:
August 19, 1946**

8
19
1946
——
1973   1 + 9 + 7 + 3 = 20 = 2

Time/Space + Priestess

Bill Clinton has Time-Space as his primary Template and the Priestess as his secondary template. The ability to see the big picture (moving himself out of horrible poverty with his vision of the future) got him the Presidency for two terms. And while he certainly has the big picture viewpoint, able to focus on major issues and ignore the details, this is exactly what got him into trouble. He was unable to realize that the details counted to other people and to acknowledge that those details were important.

New York Senator Hilary Rodham Clinton: October 26, 1947

10
26
1947
—
1983 $1 + 9 + 8 + 3 = 21 = 3$

Universe + Empress

Hilary Rodham Clinton has Universe as her primary template and the Empress as her secondary template. She has it all and knows how to get even more. She manifests what she wants very effectively and knows how to set her boundaries. Her "It Takes A Village..." work represents a classic example of how a highly functional Empress works.

Chelsea Clinton:
February 27, 1980

2
27
1980
——
2009 $2 + 9 = 11 = 2$

Strength + Priestess

Chelsea Clinton has Strength as her primary template and the Priestess as her secondary template. Chelsea certainly needed a great deal of internal Strength to get through her childhood in the public eye. Her Priestess inner-knowing allowed her to carve her own path and yet still be supportive of her parents.

Elvis Presley:
January 8, 1935

1
8
1935
——
1944 1 + 9 + 4 + 4 = 18 = 9

Moon + Hermit

Elvis had Moon as his primary template and the Hermit as his secondary template. Elvis was as changeable as the tides – in one moment, out the next. He re-invented himself over and over again. Despite his showy public persona, he seemed to prefer hiding out in his mansion and living his own internal life.

Oprah Winfrey:
January 29, 1954

1
29
1954
———
1984   1 + 9 + 8 + 4 = 22 = 4

Fool + Emperor

Oprah Winfrey has Fool as her primary template and the Emperor as her secondary template. Oprah a Fool? Absolutely! She displays all the distracting characteristics but channels them so she can share them with the world. Hosting a variety show is just about the best thing for a Fool, and her business sense and "empire-building" provide a testament to her best Emperor characteristics. She has obviously learned about sharing and delegating, two of the Emperor's worst faults turned into virtues.

Templates at Work

What happens when two or more templates get together at work? If all of you know what makes the others tick, then you all can get your jobs done much more effectively. There are several ways for templates to show up in a work environment: Manager, Employee, Customer/Client, or Salesperson. In addition, many folks are unhappy or downright miserable in jobs that stifle their souls. Knowing the right job for your Template can go a long way to happiness in the workplace, regardless of the others in the office.

The Fool at Work

Manager as Fool: Depending on the Manager's template, there could be total chaos or merely a lot of frustration in the workplace. He might be totally irresponsible, trusting that his employees will take care of it all or that everything will all "just work out." If the Manager has any discipline at all, this could be a great template for someone wanting to work in a start-up company, or start a company of his or her own. In such situations, risk-taking and the ability to change direction on a moment's notice are definitely assets.

Employee as Fool: The Fool Employee needs a lot of latitude and responds poorly to discipline, regimen or order. When needing to manage a Fool, it is best to know that the Fool's direction looks a lot like the Drunkard's Walk – a weaving line seeming to lead everywhere but to the goal. As long as the Fool is not under a time crunch, he or she eventually will get to the destination. Deadlines can turn the Fool off completely.

Customer/Client as Fool: You can only capture the Fool's attention for a little while, so you'd better be quick with your sales pitch! A generalist, the Fool becomes more interested in outside connections and universality than specs, charts and details. The good news is that the Fool generally makes up his mind quickly; the bad news is that he may never get back to you to tell you his decision, so always follow up with a Fool. Never make the mistake of equating Fool with stupid; Fools can be highly intelligent but not particularly focused.

Salesperson as Fool: The only good aspects of a Fool in sales are her enthusiasm for the product and her ability to get along with the customers. Otherwise, her ability to be distracted by a hard-luck story or some other irrelevancy will make her not worth the price of the sale.

Best Careers for a Fool: Entrepreneur, inventor, artist, think-tank member.

Worst Careers for a Fool: Desk job, rote work, factory worker, accountant.

The Magician at Work

Manager as Magician: The well-adjusted Magician Manager can make it all happen, pulling miracles out at every turn. He is likely to be hands-on, and know the job well. If the Magician is unscrupulous, he could take advantage of others on the team by performing sleight-of-hand, now-you-see-it-now-you-don't tricks.

Employee as Magician: Stand back and watch the magic happen. The Magician performs best in highly-creative jobs with lots of available resources. If the resources aren't there, the Magician will create them or make them available somehow.

Customer/Client as Magician: Watch out! The Magician as customer will probably create his own deals, work out his own combinations and tell you exactly what he wants. The dishonest Magician will show up as a con-man. (see Salesperson as Magician)

Salesperson as Magician: If it sounds too good to be true, It probably is! And whatever "it" is, the Magician will probably try to sell it to you. The Magician makes an enormously successful Salesperson. Unless the Magician operates as an independent distributor with his own inventory, he will create major problems by promising customers the moon on a silver platter just to make the sale.

Best Careers for a Magician: Marketing, sales, creative accounting, math/physics.

Worst Careers for a Magician: Rote, repetitive work with no creative potential.

The Priestess at Work

Manager as Priestess: In a word, disastrous! Since the Priestess "just knows" everything that's going on, she expects everyone around to know as well. Employees will find her incredibly frustrating. Do not expect a Priestess to conduct any kind of cross-training or write up procedures.

Employee as Priestess: The Priestess as an employee can be a difficult person with whom to work. Reports will be terse, and she will seldom ask questions. She will have her way of doing things and will only want to do things her way. She is not a team player. Her best quality as an Employee will lie in the fact that she's usually a hard worker and driven to perfectionism.

Customer/Client as Priestess: The Priestess knows what she wants, and already knows everything about it, so don't try to tell her differently. Your best strategy lies in being as knowledgeable as possible yourself and guessing (correctly!) what she desires.

Salesperson as Priestess: The Priestess generally is the most knowledgeable person on the sales team. She can be a fantastic saleswoman, because she knows that whatever product or service she's selling is the best. Thus, she will possess a simple attitude: "Why would anyone possibly want to purchase anything else?"

Best Careers for a Priestess: Psychic, researcher, analyst, stockbroker.

Worst Careers for a Priestess: Speaker, teacher/trainer, presenter.

The Empress at Work

Manager as Empress: The Empress takes care of her people, making sure they have everything they need. She might appear overwhelming to some employees, since at her worst she will want to get involved in running their personal lives as well as their professional ones.

Employee as Empress: The Empress will serve as the office Mom. She will have the candy jar on her desk and will always have an extra box of staples or paper clips ready to lend. She will work long hours for the company, but she might find herself vulnerable to office romances.

Customer/Client as Empress: When the Empress walks through the door, cheer, because she often will be your best customer. She will not only buy your product or service, but she will be the nicest, warmest person with whom you work.

Salesperson as Empress: The Empress needs to stay away from a career in sales; she will be taken in (usually) by every hard luck story, and give everything away. On the other hand, she'll be great at buttering up customers and making them feel like a million dollars.

Best Careers for an Empress: Nurse, teacher, customer service, florist.

Worst Careers for an Empress: Any career without personal interaction.

The Emperor at Work

Manager as Emperor: The Emperor can be an inspirational manager, full of ideas and energy and a can-do attitude. At his worst, he will be completely unable to delegate, or he'll go off on some wild tangent far from the company's goals as a whole. The Emperor can cause the whole team to crash in the process.

Employee as Emperor: The Emperor will not be satisfied as a worker bee. He will want the manager's job as soon as possible and will climb the ladder rapidly. He gets bored easily, so keep him busy with new projects.

Customer/Client as Emperor: You have only one short chance to catch and keep the Emperor's attention, so make your pitch quickly and make it good. Don't count on past performance to keep the Emperor loyal to you; he will only be interested in what you can do for him NOW.

Salesperson as Emperor: The Emperor needs the quick sale; he will have no patience with cultivating a customer over the long haul.

Best Careers for a Emperor: Entrepreneur, executive, "C"-level, Queen Bee.

Worst Careers for an Emperor: Any job without advancement possibilities; worker bee.

The Hierophant at Work

Manager as Hierophant: The Hierophant can be an extremely good manager, supportive and helpful in guidance. He usually inspires his employees to do their best. However, this template also can be restrictive and rule-bound beyond the point of annoyance.

Employee as Hierophant: The Hierophant will be a loyal employee and will work best in a supervisory position. However, the Hierophant doesn't always take orders well, preferring to give them instead. Be sure to have rules and procedures in place or give the Hierophant the task of creating them.

Customer/Client as Hierophant: The Hierophant will have already educated himself about your product or service, so you have very little to do in that regard. If the Hierophant has questions, prepare to be thorough and detailed with your answers.

Salesperson as Hierophant: The Hierophant's main strength as a salesperson revolves around educating the customer. This template works best when given plenty of data sheets to go over and present to clients.

Best Careers for a Hierophant: Trainer/teacher, management, Quality Assurance, lawyer/judge, minister.

Worst Careers for a Hierophant: Any management position in a start-up company, test pilot.

The Lovers at Work

Manager as Lovers: When they're healthy, the Lovers can be wonderful managers: quick decision-makers, able to delegate or to take action depending upon the situation. Otherwise, they're terrible ditherers, and if by some miracle they've gotten themselves into a management position, they depend on their direct reports to pull them out of the fire.

Employee as Lovers: The Lovers can be a joy or a royal pain to work with. If their manager is good, they'll be outstanding, but a hands-off manager with an irresolute Lover spells a disaster in the making.

Customer/Client as Lovers: The ability to make decisions remains a key issue with the Lovers in this position. At any sign of hemming and hawing, prepare for a long session or meeting. Be careful, though, about how firmly you come across; they won't stand for being bullied. Be sure to point out the contrasts between your product or service and the competition's, and make sure you've done your homework on both.

Salesperson as Lovers: The Lovers are excellent at upside/downside/otherside perspectives. Give them a product that they can compare and contrast with something else, and they will perform well.

Best Careers for Lovers (if healthy): Psychologist, data analyst, air traffic controller, mathematician.

Worst Careers for Lovers: Psychologist, air traffic controller.

The Chariot at Work

Manager as Chariot: The Chariot might not remain in a job too long and will be too restless to sit at a desk much. Other than that, the Chariot makes an excellent hands-off manager. They generally energize their staff and others around them.

Employee as Chariot: The Chariot is a go-getter and a hard worker that will willingly do overtime as long the work isn't boring. Just be aware that the grass may soon look greener to them somewhere else, and they'll be gone.

Customer/Client as Chariot: Hang on to the Chariot while you've got them. Keep any presentations short and to the point, or they'll get bored and restless.

Salesperson as Chariot: The Chariot has no patience with long sales cycles. Give them a product with quick turnover and they'll perform well.

Best Careers for a Chariot (if healthy): Delivery driver, trucker, travel planner, astronaut, jockey, traveling salesperson.

Worst Careers for a Chariot: Desk jockey, assembler.

Balance at Work

Manager as Balance: When the Balance template is doing well (when they are in Balance), they are stable, well-adjusted and excellent managers. When they're out of Balance, expect high drama all the time. Balance may perceive everything as either going extremely well or extremely badly. The catastrophe may be as real or as imaginary as Balance's outlook.

Employee as Balance: The Balance template likes well-defined duties. They can be steady or full of ups and downs.

Customer/Client as Balance: In general, Balance likes to hear both the pros and the cons of a product or service. Be as honest as possible and withhold nothing. You're more likely to get the business using this strategy.

Salesperson as Balance: If you have a business with lots of cover-ups and hidden agendas, do not hire a Balance template to sell your product or service. They will have difficulty not revealing all to their customers. If they find out you've been less than honest with them, they'll quit.

Best Careers for Balance: Accountant, math/physics, police, lawyer.

Worst Careers for Balance: Stock broker, con artist.

Hermit at Work

Manager as Hermit: Hermits are prone to management by walking around, peering over your shoulder and giving advice about how to do your job. When they're not out wandering the hallways, they're ensconced in their offices thinking of new ways of doing things "better."

Employee as Hermit: The Hermit always offers maximum productivity, so much so that his frequent need for downtime will seem a relief. The Hermit will most likely work alone but will need to report in regularly.

Customer/Client as Hermit: The Hermit will listen carefully and observe everything then probably tell you how to redesign your process from the bottom up. If you can impress him or improve his efficiency, he'll buy.

Salesperson as Hermit: The Hermit must sell products or services in which he believes. Given that, the Hermit will probably be your best salesperson.

Best Careers for Hermit: Teacher/trainer, speaker, efficiency expert, Quality Assurance.

Worst Careers for Hermit: Entrepreneur.

Fortune at Work

Manager as Fortune: The Fortune template has little order or discipline and simply handles things as they come up. As long as Fortune's employees can work independently, everything will be fine.

Employee as Fortune: She will be brilliant and erratic and completely unsuited to any kind of daily grind. She's capable of great work or really awful screw-ups depending on the opportunity offered.

Customer/Client as Fortune: There's absolutely no telling if Fortune will buy or not, but if what you're selling or offering seems like a gamble, it's more likely Fortune will want it. Be sure to either emphasize the upside or point out the offer's limited time availability.

Salesperson as Fortune: Be careful of the deals that Fortune creates to get the sale. Some ideas will be brilliant, while others will backfire.

Best Careers for Fortune: Entrepreneur, marketing, sales, gambler, stockbroker.

Worst Careers for Fortune: Accounting, assembly, any kind of rote-work.

Strength at Work

Manager as Strength: When healthy, Strength represents the perfect manager. A real leader, Strength sets a good example, works hard and encourages others. When Strength comes from her weak side, she pulls the energy of her team down and keeps it there.

Employee as Strength: As the steadiest employee, Strength anchors the center of any group. A malfunctioning Strength whines about every little thing (paper clips, staplers, or coffee) and misses the point of every meeting or project.

Customer/Client as Strength: Once Strength's mind is made up, there's no budging her. Get Strength's business, and you've got it for life. Lose it, and Strength is gone forever.

Salesperson as Strength: Strength is the one you send in for the long haul. Strength is capable of going the distance, particularly with extended sales cycles.

Best Careers for Strength: Research, sales, counseling, tech support.

Worst Careers for Strength: Anything needing quick decisions, or where the environment changes frequently.

Hanged Man at Work

Manager as Hanged Man: The Hanged Man will go to great lengths for a company and for his employees. He expects the same from them.

Employee as Hanged Man: He will give anything to a cause as long as it's worthwhile. Expect to get a minimum of 60 hours of work per week.

Customer/Client as Hanged Man: As a client, the businesses, products and services most likely to attract the Hanged Man are those that seem to be worthwhile causes. He will typically shop at health-food stores and invest in "green" stocks. At the cash register, he will put a dollar in the change collector for a cause every time.

Salesperson as Hanged Man: The Hanged Man will only work for companies who have a product or service he can believe in passionately. Therefore, he will sell just as passionately, and frequently can get clients to change their minds about whatever he is selling.

Best Careers for Hanged Man: Firefighter, police, soldier, stay-at-home mom, mathematician.

Worst Careers for Hanged Man: EMT, "ordinary" corporate job.

Death at Work

Manager as Death: Death can be a great manager, except that those working with Death can expect everything to change at least once a year. Shake-ups and reorganizations will be frequent, and no one will be immune to the changes.

Employee as Death: Do not expect Death to be at the same job for very long; change is Death's middle name. If Death stays at the same company for very long, it's only because he climbed the corporate ladder. Death will leave at the first sign of greener pastures elsewhere.

Customer/Client as Death: You might get Death as a client once, but don't expect loyalty or consistency.

Salesperson as Death: Death is an unlikely salesperson at best. Death's attitude towards selling can be voiced simply: "If you buy, you buy." If you don't buy, Death won't try to change your mind.

Best Careers for Death: Counselor (grief, addiction, or career).

Worst Careers for Death: Mortician (not enough change!), sales.

Art at Work

Manager as Art: When in a positive mode, Art will encourage creativity and have very relaxed rules. When not functioning well, Art will frown upon creativity in underlings and perceive it as threatening, so his department will be very rule-bound.

Employee as Art: The Art employee will be highly creative and expressive. Allowed free creative license, Art will get the whole department, let alone the particular job, looking better.

Customer/Client as Art: As a client, Art will want lots of options, so he can play and put his own unique spin on your product or service. Expect Art to ask questions like, "Well, what if we did it this way?"

Salesperson as Art: Art's sales will directly correlate with the flexibility and creativity of the product or service offered.

Best Careers for Art: Artist, composer, interior designer, chef.

Worst Careers for Art: The military.

Devil's Play at Work

Manager as Devil's Play: You will always find a candy jar or some kind of toy on the Devil's Play desk, but you will seldom find Devil's Play there. When you do find him, he will have a sunny demeanor but not offer much help.

Employee as Devil's Play: In this case, if Devil's Play is addicted to work, he will be at the office as close to 24/7 as he can. Otherwise, work needs to be fun to get the best out of him.

Customer/Client as Devil's Play: Find out what the Devil's Play client is attached to, and work your sales pitch around that. If he's not attached to anything, then appeal to his sense of fun and play.

Salesperson as Devil's Play: In general, Devil's Play will be popular with clients and customers. Fun loving and easy to get along with, it becomes a toss-up as to whether Devil's Play will work for a commission or not. Be aware that Devil's Play may have no problem falsifying documents in his favor.

Best Careers for Devil's Play: Elementary school teacher, animal trainer.

Worst Careers for Devil's Play: The military, medical doctor.

Tower at Work

Manager as Tower: Everything in the Tower's life is perceived as a catastrophe. There's always some kind of emergency. If you can live with a hair trigger, you'll never be bored working for the Tower.

Employee as Tower: The Tower employee is best used as a predictor of worst-case scenarios. As catastrophic thinkers, Towers will always advise that whatever you are planning or creating won't work or will fail spectacularly. Listen to what Tower says if you want ideas on how to plug holes; they're usually dead on target, but their ideas sometimes border on the absurd.

Customer/Client as Tower: When dealing with a Tower, have a good warranty or money-back guarantee handy and be prepared to have something go wrong. The Tower serves as a good beta tester for any product.

Salesperson as Tower: You might lose business hiring the Tower as a salesperson. They can't help pointing out all the flaws in your product or service to a potential customer or client. On the other hand, people are sometimes impressed by that strategy of complete honesty.

Best Careers for Tower: Actuary, insurance agent, transition team for troubled companies.

Worst Careers for Tower: Sales, nuclear engineer, air traffic control.

Star at Work

Manager as Star: When in her positive aspect, the Star manager will gently encourage everyone around her to be Stars as well. She can bring out the best in people. When in her negative aspect, however, she acts as a black hole, utterly selfish, demanding, and/or a credit thief.

Employee as Star: The Star works brilliantly. She is clear about her responsibilities to her job, her self and to others.

Customer/Client as Star: The Star will have sales folks feeling as though they've received a privilege by working with her having her as their client. However, when the Star is in her negative aspect, the nearest heads will roll.

Salesperson as Star: The Star generally will treat customers as though they are an honored guest and will probably get top sales awards regularly.

Best Careers for Star: Performer, public speaker, sales, counselor.

Worst Careers for Star: Prison guard, military.

Moon at Work

Manager as Moon: The Moon manager will keep to herself, and then suddenly reveal her agenda and expectations. She will typically speak in metaphors, so communication may be a problem.

Employee as Moon: The Moon employee will have cycles of brilliant ideas alternating with cycles of sullenness and a lack of productivity. The Moon always notices the hidden; you can't keep anything from her. Her most productive time will, of course, be the evening.

Customer/Client as Moon: It will be difficult to tell what the Moon thinks of anything. The Moon buys according to her internal cycle, so don't try to force anything on her when she's not ready for it.

Salesperson as Moon: The Moon sales person will quite often be able to appeal with surprising success to the hidden motives and desires of the client. However, the Moon will not be reliable; it's best to hire the Moon as seasonal salesperson.

Best Careers for Moon: Intelligence work; any thing where she can work quietly without notice, night shift.

Worst Careers for Moon: Performer, counselor, administration.

Sun at Work

Manager as Sun: The Sun is bright, energetic and willing to take credit for everything. He moves naturally on the fast track, so you probably won't have the Sun for a manager for long. Everything about the Sun easily can be discovered on the outside; very little is hidden and it's all intense.

Employee as Sun: If you have the Sun working for you, your best strategy lies in rewarding him frequently and in public. Otherwise, he'll have your job before morning, and, you'll have agreed to it as the best thing in the world.

Customer/Client as Sun: A pleasure to work with, if somewhat intense, Sun clients are charming and may sell you something if you're not careful.

Salesperson as Sun: The Sun will almost always be the top sales person in a company. They crave the limelight and will do almost anything to get it.

Best Careers for Sun: Actor, performer, "C"-level management, anything that puts them front and center of attention.

Worst Careers for Sun: Rigid, structured workplaces with no upward mobility; anything that requires him to keep secrets or keep out of the limelight.

Time-Space at Work

Manager as Time-Space: Time-Space will be a great manager for mapping out departments, planning future directions and explaining where everything fits into "the big picture." However, forget about asking Time-Space for help in any immediate day-to-day crisis.

Employee as Time-Space: If the job involves forecasting, long-range planning or different perspectives, Time-Space will make a great employee. Otherwise, you will spend a lot of time hauling Time-Space back into the present. Time-Space is useless with niggling little details.

Customer/Client as Time-Space: The Time-Space customer will want to know how long the warranty lasts and how to upgrade. Time-Space will prefer to purchase items that will last as close to forever as possible.

Salesperson as Time-Space: With the right product, the Time-Space salesman will be one of the best on your force. However this will be true only as long as Time-Space can discover and then explain how that product will fit into the customer's long-term goals.

Best Careers for Time-Space: Marketing, investment strategist, financial planner, life insurance sales.

Worst Careers for Time-Space: Detailed, in-the-moment work: assembly or stock clerk, for example.

Universe at Work

Manager as Universe: The Universe manager gets all the resources he needs in the just the right time and in just the right way. Usually nurturing and well balanced, Universe makes running the department truly a team endeavor and makes it look effortless as well.

Employee as Universe: The Universe employee is good at just about anything and will create a new job if the current one doesn't fit perfectly.

Customer/Client as Universe: The Universe client not only knows what she wants, it's always in stock and probably on sale.

Salesperson as Universe: The Universe template excels at getting the right product to the right customer. Never attempt to get him to oversell; it's just not in his makeup.

Best Careers for Universe: Import/export, nursery (plants), resource management, environmental science.

Worst Careers for Universe: Politics.

Templates in Love, Friendship and Family

Once upon a time, I was explaining the 21 Templates to a group of business people and their significant others. One man turned out to be a 2, the Priestess. When I defined the Priestess as one who "just knows," his spouse exclaimed, "Oh, my God! That's exactly what he says all the time – 'I just know!" The explanation went a long way toward fostering a better understanding between them. You, too, can have a better understanding of the people around you.

Fool: A Fool in love is a strange and wonderful thing. Hopeless romantics, Fools are given to sudden strange whims and gestures. Due to his impulsive nature, an unhealthy Fool is more likely to have a fling than to settle down and have a structured, long-term commitment.

Best Partners for a Fool: The Magician or Emperor can help focus passions and provide balance. Devil's Play partners would have a lot of fun with the Fool.

Least Likely Partners for a Fool: The Hierophant can be a disastrous partner, because he always wants rules and schedules.

Magician: The Magician gets along best with those who laugh at his jokes and pranks, go along with his schemes and are amazed when he pulls a rabbit out of his hat. The Magician seems smooth and polished, dazzling you with his patter. An unhealthy Magician is most likely to be found in a singles bar wearing lots of heavy gold chain and delivering the latest pick-up lines.

Best Partners for a Magician: The Fool or Devil's Play are good partners for a Magician emotionally, if not financially. Art can act as a source of focus and direction.

Least Likely Partners for a Magician: The Priestess is just no fun at all with her deadpan face and her unwillingness to be impressed. The Moon can be too moody and not spontaneous enough.

Priestess: The Priestess can be just about the most difficult partner in a relationship. She's usually introverted, a terrible communicator, condescending, and unresponsive. However, when she's well adjusted, she can be very perceptive and may posses the ability to sense what's going on both with herself and with her partner.

Best Partners for a Priestess: Balance (who pretty much gets along with anybody) refuses to get ruffled by the Priestess' mysterious communication style. The Star has her ego (good or bad) to serve as a buffer, and Time-Space can help provide a more extroverted point of view.

Least Likely Partners for a Priestess: Everyone else.

Empress: The Empress' habit of taking care of everyone makes her the most popular partner. Everyone loves the healthy Empress; she's great to be around. If the Empress is not healthy, though, she's likely to be co-dependent, unable to separate herself from others.

Best Partners for an Empress: Nearly everyone.

Least Likely Partners for an Empress: Hanged Man will get completely frustrated in his attempts at self-sacrifice, and will frustrate her in the process.

Emperor: The Emperor can get bored easily, so his partner's challenge revolves around keeping his interest. The healthy Emperor will be completely focused on building the relationship and developing long-term goals. The maladjusted Emperor will be focused on the conquest, and once the goal is reached will move on to the next one.

Best Partners for an Emperor: Strength, with a healthy Emperor, can keep the goals constantly updated. The Fool and the Magician will always amuse him.

Least Likely Partners for an Emperor: Lovers will want to know how his tricks work, and Chariot won't hang around to watch.

Hierophant: The Hierophant can be a bit of a bore romantically and may be very rule-bound as far as dating or wedding plans. However, this template can be extremely loyal and great with kids. The healthy Hierophant brings the Divine into the relationship in a very special way. The unhealthy Hierophant gets possessive and inflexible.

Best Partners for a Hierophant: Strength, as long as both are healthy.

Least Likely Partners for a Hierophant: The Priestess has a harder time than usual with the Hierophant, who wants external structure and form; the Priestess is too quiet and internal for this relationship.

Lovers: The Lovers, contrary to the name, have little or nothing to do with Love and much to do with choice and perception of opposites. In the Greek epic and tragic poem "The Iliad," the shepherd, Paris, has to make a choice between three beautiful women (two of whom are goddesses). This story symbolizes the Lovers. Classically, Lovers always perceive everything as having to do with choice, and this can drive their partners crazy.

Best Partners for Lovers: Hierophant provides structures and rules, avoiding the paralysis. Strength can also help smooth the way.

Least Likely Partners for Lovers: Chariots will want the choice made NOW or go on to something else.

Chariot: Constantly on the go, Chariots could have invented speed dating. The best ones recognize their own restlessness and change scenery rather than relationships. Unfortunately, many Chariots change their partners about as often as they change their socks.

Best Partners for a Chariot: If the Hermit or Moon and Chariot have the same internal schedules, they both can go with the flow. Balance and Star have the egos to handle the constant change.

Least Likely Partners for a Chariot: Hierophant has the least risk-tolerance. The Empress would be devastated at the Chariot's sudden moves, and the Hermit would be left behind in his cave.

Balance: Balance can be one of the best or the worst partners. Balance either gets along with anyone or goes for high drama. They can run hot and cold in a relationship or be the classic "steadying influence."

Best Partners for Balance: Almost everyone, especially the Priestess.

Least Likely Partners for Balance: When Balance gets into drama, the Tower will fall apart.

Hermit: The Hermit goes in cycles – social and great to have around one moment and impossible to find the next. Usually, Hermits emerge from their caves rejuvenated and better adjusted than when they went in. Their partners need to have an extra dose of patience during retreats.

Best Partners for Hermit: The Priestess is able to give the Hermit the quiet time he needs. The Empress would be totally supportive. If the Moon is on the same schedule of retreat and rebirth, she and the Hermit get along great.

Least Likely Partners for Hermit: Chariot, as mentioned earlier, would just leave him behind.

Fortune: Fortune's name says it all: Either Fortune is lucky in love or not. Generally, Fortune makes the most of an opportunity but has difficulty making a relationship last.

Best Partners for Fortune: Fool, Magician, and Chariot all provide a kind of balance for Fortune.

Least Likely Partners for Fortune: The Hierophant will drive Fortune crazy with rules and schedules.

Strength: Next to the Empress, Strength gets along or complements others better than the other templates. Strength's primary ability is to go within and find the internal resources to make relationships work. However, an unhealthy Strength will try to force "solutions" on her partner, which can lead to frustration and resentment on both sides.

Best Partners for Strength: Strength can encourage the Priestess to communicate and bring out her best. Strength also complements the Moon, keeping the bright side bright and the dark side merely dim.

Least Likely Partners for Strength: Tower won't accept any reassurance when they're unhealthy.

Hanged Man: The Hanged Man sees everything in a relationship in terms of sacrifice. He asks himself, "What am I giving up for you?" When he's healthy, you'll never notice the sacrifice; when not, you'll regret it. Co-dependents, beware! You have probably met your match in the Hanged Man.

Best Partners for Hanged Man: Fortune, who generally (at least half the time) has much to give back and will appreciate the Hanged Man covering for his down times.

Least Likely Partners for Hanged Man: The Empress, who won't be able to give enough; she'll go crazy tracking down to whom the Hanged Man has given the gifts she gave him.

Death: As weird as it sounds, as long as you can cope with change, you'll be able to cope with Death as a partner. When Death is healthy, the relationship will prosper and thrive because old "stuff" will constantly get pruned away. Trouble arises when Death can't get rid of outworn habits and attitudes, and they pile up in every area (physical, mental, emotional and spiritual).

Best Partners for Death: The Star and Death make a great couple, especially when they're healthy, since they bring each other to new heights.

Least Likely Partners for Death: The Hierophant can be too rigid and fond of structure to change easily.

Art: When Art is healthy, she ranks with the Empress as the best partner of all. Art's creative, vibrant nature gets everyone around her feeling alive and exuberant. Art can be a bit of a diva, however, and may exploit the "artist's temperament" to the fullest.

Best Partners for Art: The Fool and Art can resonate off of each other, pushing their creative tendencies ever higher, but they would be best off not having a romantic relationship. For romance, the Sun would help Art focus outward and provide encouragement. Balance would also suit.

Least Likely Partners for Art: The Hermit's or the Moon's moodiness will drive Art crazy.

Devil's Play: You will have more fun with a Devil's Play partner than with anyone else. No one else has as much imagination or sense of possibility. However, in a long-term, committed relationship, Devil's Play can get wearing. All fun and no work make Jack (and Jill) dull, too!

Best Partners for Devil's Play: A healthy Hierophant or Balance will set appropriate limits on Devil's Play. Unhealthy partners soon will be at each other's throats.

Least Likely Partners for Devil's Play: The Fool and Devil's Play might get along well together, but more likely they will end up hurt or in jail after too much partying.

Tower: A healthy Tower won't waste any time getting out of a bad relationship. The Tower craves tearing down structure and old ways of behaving in favor of new ones. They will more likely be in therapy – with multiple therapists – for life. Tower tends to be somewhat anxious and often worried that "something's" going to happen.

Best Partners for Tower: Chariot provides the complement to the Tower with its constant change and movement. The Tower may also tolerate the moodiness of the Hermit or the Moon a little bit better than others. Death, with his emphasis on transformation and renewal, would satisfy Tower's tastes.

Least Likely Partners for Tower: Hierophant, with his emphasis on process and long-term structure, would become frustrated with the Tower. The Priestess, with her cool denials in the face of disaster, might well be the most irritating to the Tower.

Star: A healthy Star supports her partner in every way: emotionally, mentally, physically, and even spiritually. She has grace and ease in any situation and sees the best in everyone. An unhealthy Star becomes a drama queen and behaves destructively to everyone around her. Jealous and possessive, she tolerates no competition in any arena – especially romance.

Best Partners for Star: The Fool or the Tower might benefit the most from having a relationship with the Star. Even Devil's Play could learn to avoid excess in her company.

Least Likely Partners for Star: The Sun would seek to outshine her, and unless he was very balanced would cause major frustration for both. If both the Sun and the Star were unhealthy…supernova!

Moon: The Moon's moodiness and self-preoccupation can be the worst aspects of being in a relationship with her. On the other hand, she is also the one most likely to have been through therapy and benefited from it. Chances are good that she's gotten a handle on her issues and is willing to explore them. Then, she will be focused on your issues, whether or not you have any or are ready, able and willing to deal with them.

Best Partners for Moon: The Fool and the Moon would get along very well. While the Moon needs her quiet space, the Fool would simply go off on his own adventures. The Priestess would also welcome the need to be quiet and go within. These personalities just need to remember to come out into the real world now and then.

Least Likely Partners for Moon: Chariot won't have the patience to give Moon her moods, and neither will the Tower.

Sun: The Sun needs to be the dominant and visible partner in a relationship. The hit of the party, Sun will make an entrance and gather everyone around to worship him. Anyone wishing to be in a relationship with the Sun needs to know the Sun always comes first. But you can't help loving him anyway.

Best Partners for Sun: Devil's Play would have a lot of fun with the Sun and wouldn't get jealous.

Least Likely Partners for Sun: The Priestess will exasperate him because she won't respond to his magnetic pull. Sun will have no patience with Tower's disasters, since Sun believes nothing bad can ever happen to him.

Time-Space: Time-Space probably celebrates more 60- or 70-year anniversaries than anyone else. If you're looking for a long-term relationship, look no further. Also, Time-Space would have been voted "Least Likely to Have a One Night Stand." You will never find Time-Space in a pickup bar unless connected to a longitudinal study on dating habits. Unfortunately, all this great long-term vision makes it difficult to deal with him in the Now.

Best Partners for Time-Space: The Priestess, oddly enough, provides balance for the here and now. The Star can also be relied upon to gently bring Time-Space's vision back to Earth. Time-Space provides a good counter to the Fool's short-sightedness.

Least Likely Partners for Time-Space: The Sun would demand "look at me now!" Time-Space would reply, "Sure...in a minute."

Universe: The Universe will always manifest the perfect partner at the time. And when that partner isn't perfect, some overriding reason will arise for that partner to leave and for a new one to appear. The best partner of all is a healthy Universe, since Universe always brings the best of everything and the smoothest path.

Best Partners for Universe: Literally everyone can be with the Universe; it just depends on what Universe's needs are at that moment.

Least Likely Partners for Universe: What Universe's not looking for at the time.

Money Templates

How do you handle your money? Some of your attitudes about money are inherited from your family and culture, and you are born with others that may go completely against your upbringing.

Fool: As you may guess, the Fool could care less about money. If he's got it, he spends it. (You may have heard of the phrase, "A fool and his money are soon parted.") Here's the good news: If the Fool doesn't have money, it doesn't bother him a bit. The best idea for a Fool is to hire an accountant.

Magician: The Magician can create money out of thin air. He is incredibly creative about getting money, making money and, in particular, getting your money. The Magician doesn't get stressed about money, because there's always more coming.

Priestess: The Priestess can use her intuition to invest in stocks or anything where having a bone-deep knowledge would be an advantage. However, for the most part, she remains indifferent to money; if it's there, she'll use it, and if it's not, she doesn't seem to miss it.

Empress: As the archetype of the creative principle, the Empress embodies prosperity. In households where the Empress rules, even when there is seemingly a lack of money, a feeling of richness and abundance exists. The Empress plants seeds and nurtures them. When she reaps the harvest, she frequently gives generously to others.

Emperor: The Emperor is full of big ideas. He might start with a small amount of money, but he'll end up with a big heap – if he can stay the course.

Hierophant: In the best case scenario, the Hierophant learns everything about finance well enough to teach it. The worst case scenario arises when he can't live what he learns.

Lovers: The Lovers' archetype revolves around decisions and choices. When their psyche is healthy, the financial decisions are sound; when the Lovers are indecisive, beware. The Lovers dither horribly and will frequently miss opportunities to make money.

Chariot: The Chariot is interested in anything that promises immediate – or faster – returns. Hang on to your hat if you invest in anything the Chariot has going on.

Balance: When it comes to money, Balance represents the best and the worst of the templates. Balance is the best at – no surprise - balancing a checkbook and is possibly the most organized, but Balance also may find himself constantly broke, recovering financially or with finances (along with everything else) in utter chaos.

Hermit: The Hermit will build and build his nest egg, and then go out and spend it in one spectacular binge. Sometimes, Hermits only are revealed as millionaires when their wills are read.

Fortune: The Fortune template can be a gambler and enormously successful when the timing is right. Fortune always knows when the luck has run out, and when to grab the brass ring.

Strength: The Strength template has the steadiness to build a nest egg and the discipline to use it appropriately.

Hanged Man: The Hanged Man's essential personality revolves around sacrifice. Beware, if you live with a Hanged Man. Know that the next sob-story the Hanged Man hears will receive his very last penny.

Death: From extreme to extreme, when it comes to money it's all or nothing for Death. Don't rely on Death to have money, since Death's situation is always changing.

Art: When it comes to making money, creative endeavors work best for the Art template, but Art needs control and sometimes even a keeper; Art would be best off hiring a bookkeeper or accountant to manage his money.

Devil's Play: If Balance has the best money template, Devil's Play has the worst. Devil's Play is subject to addictions, and money can be one of the things to which they become addicted. If not attached to money, they are fun to be around since they always seem to have enough to share with everyone.

Tower: The Tower lives from catastrophe to catastrophe, rarely finding himself without a situation that takes away his money or property.

Star: The Star is aware of what she's worth and gets it: no more and no less.

Moon: Like the Hermit, the Moon has cycles of spending and saving. Sometimes, Moon finds money that she doesn't even remember hiding!

Sun: The Sun generates prosperity, and everyone always knows how much money he possesses. He is generous, gives to friends, and tithes richly.

Time-Space: Time-Space invests in long-term investments like bonds and CDs. When it comes to money, Time-Space needs to learn how to afford to put dinner on the table right now, today.

Universe: Deeply connected to everything, the Universe manifests exactly what he or she needs in the right time and place.

Forecasting with the Templates

Just like people, days have personalities, too. Have you ever had a day where it seemed like you were traveling to and fro constantly? It was probably a Chariot day. Or maybe you experienced a day when nothing went right (Tower) or everything did (Universe). You can forecast the theme of every day of the year just by adding up the numbers of the day, just as you did for your birthday. Of course, attitude and belief play a huge part in the character and experiences of your life; if you expect catastrophe at every turn, you may well get it no matter what day it is!

What kind of day are you going to have? The descriptions below focus only on the positive aspects of the day. Anyone can have a bad day...

Fool: A happy-go-lucky kind of day. Be aware of opportunities coming your way.

Magician: Today is a day to make things happen: cut a deal, create something new, take action.

Priestess: You should make the time to do some internal work today. Meditate, or at least pay attention to your intuition.

Empress: The day has the potential to be incredibly productive. Harvest what you have planted in the past.

Emperor: Go out and conquer the world today. Expand your territory; increase your surroundings.

Hierophant: Learn something new today. What is it that you've always wanted to know? This is a good day to do research.

Lovers: Yes, on Lovers' day, make love, if you can. At the very least, notice and appreciate the people in your life.

Chariot: You won't be standing still much today. Plan to run errands or travel today.

Balance: If you work today, try to get some playtime in as well. Or, if it's a play day, do some work. If you're active, plan some quiet time. If you're meditating, find some time to laugh or shout out loud.

Hermit: This will be a day when you're allowed or you allow yourself to retreat inside your shell and pay attention to yourself.

Fortune: Pay attention to your finances today as well as to any opportunities that may come along.

Strength: Be aware of your hidden resources. Where does your power come from? How do you use it?

Hanged Man: Look at things from a different perspective today. Walk in another's moccasins for a mile or so.

Death: Today, do something completely different, something you've never done before.

Art: Let your creative juices flow. Put things together and shake them up just to see what happens.

Devil's Play: Discover something you haven't done since you were a child that you really enjoyed doing, and do it.

Tower: Take that step you've been putting off. Practice reverse procrastination.

Star: Allow yourself to shine today. Take proper credit. Accept compliments gracefully.

Moon: Take a look inside yourself and discover any hidden incentives or motivations. You don't necessarily have to take action, but know what's gestating inside.

Sun: Put yourself in the limelight. Be active, and be present.

Time-Space: Take the long view: What will it be like a week, a month, a year, a decade from now. This is a good day to set goals.

Universe: Just know that everything you wish for will come true – you just have to believe.

Putting it all Together

In the first chapter, a template was defined as something "used as a starting point." Obviously, human personalities are much more complicated than can be laid out in a single, short book. Whole libraries exist, full of personality explorations; we are endlessly fascinated with why we are the way we are. Use the Templates as a starting point to understand yourself a little better. Use them to add to your observations about others.

One particularly astute gentleman, after hearing the first ten Templates described, said "But it seems like I have a little bit of all of them in me!" He is correct – we all act like Fools at some point in our lives, Hermits at others; our focus can be inward like the Priestess, or far ahead like Time-Space.

To achieve your best, integrate all the positives from all the Templates, and be aware when the negative aspects show up. When we are conscious of our own talents and limitations, and can accept them as such, our lives and the lives of those around us become richer and more meaningful.

CPSIA information can be obtained
at www.ICGtesting.com
Printed in the USA
FSOW02n1141261015
12467FS